Thoughts and Prayers for Families

Lionel & Patricia Fanthorpe

GW00707425

BISHOPSGATE PRESS

This book is dedicated to our beloved daughters,
Stephanie and Fiona, Maurice and Iain, our much
loved sons-in-law, Zac and Katie, our adored
grandchildren: and all our family everywhere.

© 2001 Lionel & Patricia Fanthorpe

British Library Cataloguing in Publication Data
Fanthorpe, Lionel and Patricia
Thoughts and Prayers for Families

All enquiries and requests relevant to this title
should be sent to the publisher Bishopsgate
Press Ltd., Bartholomew House, 15 Tonbridge
Road, Hildenborough, Kent TN11 9BH.

Printed by Lanes Ltd.,
16 Patricia Way, Pysons Road Industrial Estate,
Broadstairs, Kent CT10 2LF.

Contents

Foreword
by Canon Stanley Mogford, MA

It has been my privilege, for many years now, to read before anyone else, the many books that have come from the 'Fanthorpe Partnership'. They have entrusted me with writing a Foreword before each of the books could go to the publishers. During the last few years some twenty of their manuscripts have come my way.

Every book has left me marvelling at the depth and quality of the work. How can it be possible for anyone to write at such speed, on subject matter so diverse, and always with care, insight and ease? The research alone involved in the two books, The Oak Island Mystery with its tale of treasure sought over generations by many but found by none, and Rennes-le-Château with its account of the exciting search for the source of the mysterious wealth that came somehow into the hands of the parish priest, Bérenger Saunière, would have been enough to defeat most of us lesser mortals.

This small book, however, will have come easier than some of the others. It concerns the family. Much that Lionel writes here comes readily from the heart of a loving marriage, forty years and more, and with loyal, devoted children to share it. The words of Charles Dickens about another marriage seem to say it all:--

"They were happy, well pleased with one another and contented with the time."

Lionel writes here of what he knows. His longing is that all families could be as Blessed as his has been.

Sadly, the facts say otherwise. Not all families are complete or happy. Perhaps they never were. Tolstoy once wrote:--

"All happy families are alike: each unhappy family is unhappy in its own way."

Some parents, for example, look on almost with disbelief at the way other people's children remain so loving and do so well. They are left wondering where they went wrong that they so alienated the affections of their sons or daughters, causing heartache for them all. Many children, these days, envy their peers who have two parents, both of whom are there for them, when they need help or encouragement. There are those who feel trapped inside a family where there is no understanding, and almost daily conflict. Others have lost altogether all family roots and affections and look to strangers to relieve their loneliness.

Lionel knows, first from his years as a schoolmaster, and subsequent years as a parish priest, how broken family can be, how rooted grief and distrust are in all too many lives. Lionel himself, in his introduction, puts it bluntly and with shaming accuracy:--

"The better things are when they go as God intended, the worse they can be when they go wrong."

This book will help many of us. It will persuade those who have good homes and a good family life never to take any of it for granted. It is a thing most precious, denied to many, and needs love and care to preserve it. It will help many of those whose family life is in turmoil. Wherever it is of use, in matters great or small, Lionel and Patricia Fanthorpe will deem themselves well Blessed, and their time on this work rewarded. Not all books have it in them to say something to the human condition. This book seeks to do it in every page and many will be glad they read it.

Canon Stanley Mogford
Cardiff, 2001

Introduction

From the lives of the Patriarchs in the Book of Genesis to Mary, Joseph and the baby Jesus on their journey from Bethlehem to Egypt, the Bible is filled with accounts of families, their struggles and their adventures. The God-given human family at its best is one of the closest observation posts to Heaven: a simple, earthly model to help us to understand the Divine Love with which God blesses us all without limit and without end.

The better things are when they go as God intended, the worse they can be when they go wrong. Christ Himself testified that He saw the fall of Lucifer, who had once been a bright and powerful heavenly servant of God. Being close to the people you love most - and who love you deeply in return - is a foretaste of Heaven itself. Being at the receiving end of the stresses and tensions of a home full of people whom you don't understand, and who don't understand you or each other - can be one of life's worst and most damaging experiences.

We've already been together for over forty eventful, exciting and adventurous family years - and we're looking forward eagerly to the next forty. We've been saddened by the loss of parents and grandparents, and an elder brother and sister, but overjoyed to have had the privilege of sharing our children's company as they grew up, and to welcome our sons-in-law and grandchildren into this growing family.

We also think that with God's help we may have learnt one or two useful things along the way. We hope that passing them on could provide some small help and encouragement for the friends who do us the honour of reading this book.

The first idea is to try to be a God-centred family - which also means making an effort to be Love-centred. The Love which Christ taught by words and by example was a totally unselfish Love, far surpassing the best of which any of us is capable. We can't get within a million light years of the standard He set, but we must always go on trying.

In the physical universe, we see the marvels and mysteries of God's power in the incomprehensible minuteness of sub-atomic particles, as well as in the unimaginable distances of inter-galactic space. The power of love can reveal itself like that in the tiniest things as well as in the greatest ones. You can leap into a raging sea or a blazing inferno to rescue someone you love at any cost: you can also tie a shoelace, fetch a cup of tea or read to them. Family love shines just as brightly in the small daily things as in the major sacrifices.

The second thing is to try to see things from the other family member's point of view. Being older does not make you wiser - neither does it make you any less wise. Make a real and consistent effort to think yourself into the other person's situation: try to imagine what it's like to be Grandfather with arthritis and two walking sticks, longing to go to the Reference Library on the far side of the city. Try to get inside the disappointment of the ten year old Rugby fanatic Grandson who didn't quite make the School Team, the seven year old Granddaughter who didn't get asked to be Aunty's bridesmaid when she'd dreamt of nothing else for weeks.

Thirdly, always follow through. Be a positive thinker and a positive doer. Be a man or woman of *action* -- no matter how long it takes to make things go right for the family you love -- make the good things you've promised really happen for them. You're never too old or too young to have the ambition, determination and success of Alexander the Great. Happiness and success are not correlated with age. Your love for your family can become your major incentive. No matter how old or how young you are, you can achieve great things for them. Because they love you, they want you to be happy. Because you love them, you want them to be happy. Because God loves all of us, He wants us all to be happy. There is no purer prayer, nor more acceptable form of worship, than the giving of happiness to God's children in His Name and for His sake. Plan good and loving things for your family - and carry them out against every obstacle. God gave you your will power. He wants you to use it well.

Fourthly, be an integrated, progressive, *learning* family -- don't just keep up: keep in front. Never be insular, or withdrawn - be involved in one another's newest interests and in the wider world. Once upon a time fire, the wheel, and the bow and arrow were strange new inventions which traditionalists had a hard job to understand. You and your family can learn to handle e-mails and the Internet, just as easily as our great-grandparents learned to cope with telephones and radios. Trust God - and then trust yourself and your family. He is the Ultimate Infinite Creative Genius, and He *made* you and your family. His Divine Craftsmanship will never let you down.

Finally, be a friendly, inclusive and open family. Always make others welcome. Adopt them and love them as if they were your own flesh and blood. Serve God in all of human society as well as in your own home.

The whole of humanity is God's family, and family life is a glorious adventure. Go for it - and God will go with you.

Lionel and Patricia Fanthorpe, Cardiff, 2001

What is a Family?

You are part of a family even if you have no living relatives in the conventional sense. You are a child of God, with billions of brothers and sisters. You have the most loving Parent and the largest family possible. In God's sight we all belong to Him and to one another. That's the first and most important family relationship.

An earthly family is a group of people who belong to one another and who love one another. That's the kind of family which the Church aims to be. Love is the criterion. Ancestry and inherited genes are only secondary considerations. When there is one human being who means more to you than your own life, you have a family. That kind of love is the first rung on God's ladder to the eternal and abundant life which Christ came to bring us.

A family is the golden frame in which our self-portraits are kept safe. A family is the train in which we travel from each of life's stations to the next. A family is the springboard from which we dive into the pool of life. A family is the treasure chest we carry, and the staff on which we lean when we are weary. A family is the communal kitchen where we give, receive and share out our essential spiritual and emotional nourishment. Your family is your special Regiment in God's army.

The Family Poem

The strong man resting in his fireside chair,
The grey-haired lady with her magazine,
He dug their garden all that afternoon,
While she was buying Christmas gifts and cards.
Their son is in the kitchen, brewing tea
For mother fetching children back from school:
They're home! And Granddad takes them on his knee
While Grandma drops her magazine and tunes
Their Cartoon Cable Channel on TV.
A hug, a kiss, a smile - hearts full of love.
This is the family. God loves them all.
Angels rejoice to share their happiness.

The Family Prayer

Great Father of all families, most wise and loving Lord, help us to understand that what we love most in those we love most is only a pale reflection of Your Glorious Loveliness. Their kindness and unselfishness, their care and devotion, is just one tiny spark from your eternal flame of grace and mercy.

Teach us to understand that a good and loving human family is only a faint shadow of that glorious fellowship which saints and angels enjoy with You in Heaven.

Help us so to obey Christ's law of love, and care for one another in our earthly families now, that, at the last, both we and they may be partakers of the everlasting joys of Your Eternal Kingdom. We ask it for the sake of Christ our Lord.

Amen.

Children

A great sculptor can look at a block of marble and see the graceful dolphin, horse or unicorn which lies hidden inside the stone, and which the rest of us cannot see until the marble has been cut away to reveal it. A loving and perceptive family can sometimes see a growing child with the eyes of a sculptor: they have a fair idea of what that boy or girl will grow up to be.

Unlike the passive form of a stone horse inside its marble block, the young adult struggling to emerge from childhood is a dynamic, thinking being with a personality and ideas of her own. The family's task is not to mould the child, but to *equip and enable* him or her to cope with life. Grandparents, parents and guardians, aunts, uncles, older brothers and sisters are not there to impose their will on the child, but to help the growing person to develop in his or her own unique way.

There are two equal and opposite horrors which adults can impose upon the young people in their care: one is neglect and unconcern - the other is to try to force them to be miniature copies of us instead of enlarged versions of their real selves.

Children's Poem

In Nazareth, in Galilee,
Young Jesus slept on Mary's knee.
He played there in the village street,
With smiling face and sandalled feet.
His earthly guardians watched him grow
Knowing that some day He would go
To where his Mission called Him on:
His carefree childhood soon be gone.
So make the most of each young day --
Youth is a friend who cannot stay.
Inside the oldest - no regret -
The child you were is living yet.
Re-live your youth, and as you do -
Think how God's Son knew childhood too.

The Children's Prayer

Blessed Lord Jesus, You were once a child like the children in our family, like we were ourselves - and as we still are deep inside.

Remind us, gracious Lord, of how much You love children, and how precious they are to You. Help us to treat them as you would treat them - to bless them, love them, protect them and help them to be themselves.

Help us to teach them about You and the way that You want them to grow up. Help us to teach them about life, so that they may live as members of Christian families. Prevent us from trying to turn them into something they don't want to be. Remind us that we are here to help and encourage them to be the best that they can be -- but in their own special, unique, individual ways - not ours.

Help us to set them an example of love, unselfishness and caring companionship.

We ask it in the Name of Him who welcomed and blessed all children, Jesus Christ, our Lord.

Amen.

Parents

There is an awesome parallel between the work of God Himself, and the responsibilities of parents. The creative aspect of parenthood reflects the creative power of God. He brought this entire universe into being in the very beginning -- God was God before He made Time and Space for us to occupy. That's another parent parallel: parents can control and understand things that their children don't yet know about. Toddlers don't know how Mum puts the new batteries in the cuddly toy frog that hops and ribbits - but they know that Mum knows, and they love playing with their frog.

The ideal parent loves, guides, protects, helps and teaches the child -- as God does on an infinitely larger scale. Human parents cannot be there all the time, no matter how much they want to be - but God is always there. We may not be aware of Him all the time, but He is always aware of us, and the nature of His Divine Awareness is Pure and Perfect Love.

The ideal parent always helps the child to the limit of his or her human ability - but even the highest and widest human ability, and the greatest determination, has its limits. There are no limits to God's ability. There is nothing which can defeat His perfect purpose.

The Parent's Poem

Help me, great Lord, to do it all,
To feed and wash them while they're small,
To clean their teeth, and try my best,
With clothes and diet and the rest,
To show those who have just begun
That life on Earth can be great fun:
With toy shops, pantomimes and fairs,
With Goldilocks and her three bears . . .
To help with all they hope to do
But most of all to turn to You,
And with Your help, to show to them
The Holy Child of Bethlehem
In all His radiant love and beauty -
Then I'll have done my parent's duty.

The Parent's Prayer

Great Lord and Father, help us as parents to become channels for Your Spirit of Love and Guidance as we do our best to help our own children. Give us the strength and wisdom to guard them, teach them, help them and enjoy their fellowship. May we always be flexible and responsive to their changing needs, so that those in our care who began as tiny babes in our arms will grow up to become our loyal and loving adult companions. Help us to express our love and appreciation of one another, and in so doing obey your perfect law of love.
We ask it for the sake of Christ our Lord.
Amen.

Grandparents and Great-Grandparents

One of the dearest wishes of the Old Testament patriarchs was to live to see their beloved children's children grow up - and many of them achieved it. In a world full of God's great and glorious gifts, few things can bring more joy. Thousands of years after the time of Abraham, Isaac and Jacob, all that is best in human nature has not changed. We can share with those biblical patriarchs the pure delight of simply being with our grandchildren, and great-grandchildren. Those who can stride with a joyful smile across the so-called generation gap have so much to give to one another. The young ones carry a special medicine compounded of enthusiasm, excitement, smiles and laughter which heals the wounds that time has inflicted on the older members of their family. The older members of the team carry a special medicine compounded of knowledge, experience and wisdom which teaches, guides and protects the young ones whom they cherish so much. Both these healing elixirs have love as their main ingredient.

Each needs the other. Each gives to the other. Each rejoices in the fellowship of the other. The Gospels do not record that Jesus ever met Mary's mother, but it would be good to think that he did, and that she was richly blessed by taking her Divine Grandson into her loving arms.

The Song of the Generations

It seems like only yesterday
That I was small like you.
Or was it just this morning
Mum and dad were children too?
I don't know where the time has gone
Nor where the years have flown.
I used to be a child, but now -
Grandchildren of my own!
We're playing in the Wendy house,
And by the paddling pool.
This morning you were in your pram -
But now you're off to school.
Next stop is university,
And then to work you'll go:
The clocks spin faster every year
As Time draws back his bow.
Let's make the most of here and now
Nor wait for work, nor weather,
But pray for all the time we can
Enjoy God's world together.

A Grandparent's Prayer

Thank You most loving Lord, for the love that leaps
the generations and brings young and old together in
fun and fellowship. Help us to be real friends and
companions, although the years seem to divide us.
Help us to understand each other, and to remember
that You are the God of Eternity, so that the passing
years are nothing in your sight. Teach us to forget our
anxieties about the passing of time, and to concentrate
on each moment, each hour and each day - so that we
may fill the eternal *now* with that love, joy and
fellowship which You intend us to have. We ask it in
the name of Him Who came so that we could have life,
and have it *abundantly*, Jesus Christ, our Lord.
Amen.

Uncles and Aunts

We should never under-estimate the God given influence of good and loving aunts and uncles. When I was a boy - over fifty years ago - I had one particular favourite uncle, my father's younger brother Hugh, who won my undying respect, affection and admiration by treating me as an adult and an equal. Sadly, he died when I was only twelve, but happy memories of his kindness must have hibernated snugly in my subconscious. When I joined the Phoenix Timber Group in Rainham, Essex, as their Industrial Training Manager, some twenty-odd years after Hugh's death, I was warmly welcomed by Malcolm Rickards, Head of their Timber Preservation Division, and we remained staunch friends all the time that I served with the Group. It was not until I looked through some old family photographs that I realised Malcolm bore an uncanny resemblance to Uncle Hugh as he had looked in his younger days when I was a boy. I concluded that it was probably because - as a newcomer to the Group --I had approached Malcolm with the same happy enthusiasm that I had felt when I had approached Uncle Hugh, that Malcolm and I had become such good friends. The kindness of a good and loving uncle in childhood laid the foundation for a valued adult friendship. The seeds of kindness always grow, although they may take years to bear fruit.

A Poem for Aunts and Uncles

There are loving aunts and uncles,
Parents' sisters, parents' brothers,
But as well as blood relations
Most of us have several others.
There's the friendly, helpful lady
Who packs baskets at the till.
There's the kind and caring neighbour
Who runs errands when we're ill.
There's the uncle at the garage
Who helps out when cars go wrong.
There's the cheerful uncle-postman
With his whistle and his song.
These adopted aunts and uncles
Make the world a better place -
Everyone feels so much happier
When we see a smiling face.

Aunts' and Uncles' Prayer

If I don't see my own family today, Lord, my own loving nephews and nieces, help me to be the best sort of adopted aunt or uncle I can be to those I do meet. We are all Your children, Lord, Your human family, and we know that it pleases You when we are kind and helpful to one another. Teach us to treat all people as Your children, and to do our best to be kind, loving and helpful to them for Your sake.

We ask it in the Name of Him Who always helped and welcomed everyone in need, Jesus Christ our Lord.

Amen.

Cousins

Because *Fanthorpe* is an unusual name, when we meet other members of the clan in different parts of the UK - or the world itself, for that matter - we usually discover after a few minutes' chat that we're cousins. Much of the old terminology such as first cousins, second cousins, or cousins twice removed isn't used much any more -- and we're not sufficiently skilled genealogists to work it out accurately anyway. But it's always a pleasure to make the acquaintance of our distant cousins, and to find from comparing our family trees that their eighteenth century ancestor, Henry, was ours as well.

When we were young, a visit from our cousins - or going to see them -- was something to look forward to: the best tea-cups came out of the cupboard, instead of the mugs we used every day. We made a bit of an effort - and so did they. That's something we might all try to do more often now, when life seems almost *too* busy, and everything accelerates all the time. Whether they're real cousins or adopted cousins, let's try to make time now and again, meta-phorically to get the best tea-cups out for people, give them our full attention, put the next pressing piece of work on the back-burner for an hour or two and really enjoy being together.

Cousins' Poem

Hi, cousins!
You're my half-way house:
Best of both worlds,
As relatives *and* friends -
Great rôle to fill!
Not *quite* a brother
Sharing everything --
Each game and sport,
Each victory and defeat --
Not *quite* a sister,
Helping me to learn
My sines and cosines -- and Pythagoras --
The week before examinations loomed.
My well loved cousins, always there for me,
And, when you want me, I am there for you.

A Cousin's Prayer

Loving Lord of every member of every family, whether we are close or far apart, help us to play our cousins' rôles to the best of our ability. Although as cousins we are not quite the same as brothers and sisters, help us to love, help and support one another as though we were. Keep us mindful of our family ties, and proud of them. Help us to keep in touch with one another, and to be genuinely caring, concerned and sympathetic in those practical ways that the Good Samaritan taught us. Let us never be too busy to remember Christmases, anniversaries and birthdays, and to send postcards as reminders of our affection when we're away on holiday. Help us, as cousins, to be relatives as well as friends, and to give the best of both kinds of love, through Jesus Christ our Lord.
Amen.

The Extended Family

The extended family can grow just as far as we want it to - and as loving Christians, members of God's great family, the Church, we should want it to grow to infinity. The extended family diagram can be seen in the shape of a cross - the central symbol of our faith. The vertical part of the cross could represent the extension of our family through time: grandparents, parents and children. The horizontal arms of the cross represent brothers, sisters and cousins - and their loving wives and husbands who have joined the family by marriage. The wider a plant can spread its roots, the stronger and healthier that plant becomes: the wider an extended family can spread, the stronger and healthier that family becomes. Just as the leaves, the stems, the roots and flowers of a plant all perform different vital functions for the welfare of the plant as a whole, so the different members of the extended family can sustain and reinforce one another for the good of the family as a whole. We can all play our part in helping to hold the extended family together by loving and caring for all the other members. We should willingly accept our duties and responsibilities towards one another - as well as enjoying the many privileges of membership of an extended family.

The Extended Family Poem

From earliest times we trace our line
Through many a generation.
God guided and sustained us then
Through tears or jubilation.
Our ancestors all turned to Christ
Their glorious Saviour hailing -
In all of life's vicissitudes
They found His love unfailing.
So we today stretch forth our hands
To cousin, sister, brother
And know that Christ rejoices in
Our love for one another.

The Extended Family Prayer

Loving Lord of the entire human race, help us to understand that the greatest extended family of all covers the whole of Your Earth. Help us to learn to love all of Your children everywhere and to think of them as our brothers, sisters and cousins. May we begin to learn this greater love by learning first to understand our own extended family. Help us to cross the gulf of years that can divide the generations, so that - whatever our ages - we can be as one. Help us to reach out to those distant members of our family whom we do not meet as often as we would like to. Remind us especially that the sick, the frail, the poor, the lonely, the troubled or afflicted members of the family need us most. Inspire us to seek them out and help them, that in so doing we may do Your will, for the sake of Jesus Christ our lord.

Amen.

The Nuclear Family

When I'm teaching my science students, we often study atomic theory together and talk about the protons and neutrons in the nucleus with the electrons in their energy levels, or shells, outside it. The nucleus lies at the very heart of the atom. When we're working on biology instead of physics, we look at the nucleus which controls the living cell. Once again, the all-important nucleus is at the heart of things - the essential inner core. In the same way, the nuclear family of parents and children is at the centre of every strong and healthy society. The closer the members of each nuclear family are to one another, the more deeply and unselfishly parents and children love one another and stay loyally together, the better it is for the communities of which those nuclear families are essential parts. Think about bricks or stones in the walls of a sturdy house. Each nuclear family is like one of those. Strong bricks and firm stones make a durable house. The cement of an extended family and the happy, integrated community life all around, hold our nuclear families together. The loving and supportive nuclear family is where we first learn to be people. The strength and security of the good nuclear family gives us the confidence to go out into the wider world and make a success of our adventures there -- knowing that our family is there to come home to.

The Nuclear Family Poem

God bless our home and family,
Mum and Dad and children too.
Be with us to protect us, Lord,
In everything we do.
Go with us when we travel, Lord,
And stay with us at home:
You are the God of Everywhere
Wherever we may roam.
Be with us in our working time;
Be with us when we play.
Be with us through the darkest night
And through the brightest day.
Be with us as the years roll by,
Then grant that we may be
With You, forever, gracious Lord,
Throughout eternity.

The Nuclear Family Prayer

Blessed Lord Jesus, You knew the joys of family life as you grew up in Nazareth. Teach us to live in peace and love together in our family, as You experienced the peace and love of growing up with Mary and Joseph. Show us how to be gentle, kind and considerate to one another - as You were to them. Teach us compassion and understanding for all the members of our family who live and work together under this one roof. Show us that in the close, loving unity of happy family life we can experience a genuine foretaste of heaven. Help us to enjoy one another's company, and to make the most of our work and leisure time together as a united family. We ask it in and through your precious Name.
Amen.

The Single Parent Family

Some single parents have gone through the grief and trauma of losing a greatly loved husband or wife. They take on the rôle of the partner who has gone before them to be with God, as well as their own. For other single parents, a once-loving relationship has failed to work out over time. We're only human. We all make mistakes and errors of judgement. God alone is perfect -- and His perfection makes merciful allowances for our frequent weaknesses and failures. He helps us to pick up the pieces and make a new start. He wants parents who are struggling alone to do the best they can to give their children double value, to be father as well as mother. Whatever the cause, the single parent needs all the loving help and support which family and friends can give. God is always there. He never leaves us. Christ never forsakes us. The Holy Spirit is continuously with us. An awareness of this constant presence of God can be a great comfort and reinforcement for the struggling single parent. God cares for you, guards you, guides you and protects you, just as you do your best to guard, guide and protect the children you love. As they turn to you, so you can turn to Him. You would never let them down: He will never let you down.

The Single Parent's Poem

There was a strange Greek legend, long ago,
Which told how giant Atlas held the world
Upon his massive shoulders, where its weight
Was all that his colossal frame could stand.
Sometimes we feel as Atlas must have felt
When all the weight of our loved children's world
Rests upon us. Alas! We are no giants,
We're flesh and blood sustained by will and love.
And when we feel the load is just too much
We turn to God -- infinite power of God -
Who holds the universe in one vast hand.
He smiles with understanding care and shares
Our much-loved burden till our strength returns.

The Single Parent's Prayer

Most loving Lord, eternal but invisible Companion of my loneliness and stress, be there to listen when I have no-one else to talk to. Comfort and strengthen me as I try to do my best to comfort and strengthen my children. Guide and help me, as I try to guide and help them. I know that You always listen caringly to me, and that You always understand my problems. Help me to be caring and understanding when I listen to them. I know that I matter to You. Help me to show my children how much they matter to me. I ask it in the name of Jesus, Who always made children welcome, even when he was tired.
Amen.

United Families

My father's first wife, Elizabeth, died in 1933, after they'd been together long enough to celebrate their Silver Wedding. My mother, Greta, was his second wife, and so when I was born in 1935 I already had a half-brother and sister and three nephews who were all older than I was! We were really two families welded together by my father's second marriage, and as a united family we all got on well. Those of us remaining on this Earth are still very happy when we get the chance to be together. It's a wonderful thing when families can be united by marriage in that kind of way. There's so much that we can learn from one another, and so much help that we can give to one another. But it needs a bit of effort, too. We all have slightly different expectations, ambitions and aspirations: different hopes, different fears and different plans. The human mind is like a parachute - it only works when it's open. We have to be open-minded and receptive when we suddenly find ourselves part of a united family. Some cherished old prejudices may have to go. Some previously unquestioned views may have to be changed in the light of new knowledge. It's all part of growing up and growing together. The central things never need to be changed: love and understanding, unselfishness and cheerfulness, and the vital ingredient of mutual respect.

United Family Poem

Your ways and ours are not the same,
Yet we must learn to be
Adopted members of just one
United family.
We'll try our best to learn from you --
And teach you what we know.
It won't be easy all the time -
But we can make it go.
Let's always do our best to help
And comfort one another:
Yesterday's stranger soon becomes
My sister or my brother.
God loves us all - no matter what
Our colour, race or clan -
His mighty family includes
Each woman and each man.

United Family Prayer

Most Loving and understanding God, You made us all, and You know us better than we know ourselves. You know all our similarities and differences. You know every detail of our individual characters. Help us to understand ourselves better, and as we look deeply into our own minds and hearts with your help, may we gain a clearer understanding of the other members of this united family. Help us always to be friendly and concerned, caring and helpful. Teach us when we are needed and welcome, and save us from intruding or being a nuisance. Help our united family to grow ever closer together, and in so doing to reflect Your love.

Amen.

Working Together

Some people experience misgivings at the thought of working with family members as well as living together in the same family home. But when we truly love someone, the more time we can spend with them, the happier we are. In our radio, TV and show-business work, Patricia's my sole agent, manager, publicity and PR executive. In our researching, lecturing and writing she's my fellow investigator and co-author. She's also my partner in our management consultancy practice and tutorial work - as well as my wife. We always work together - most days we work a twenty hour shift - and we enjoy our working lives as much as our family life and leisure.

In biblical times, families worked together. In medieval times families worked together. Before the Industrial Revolution replaced the system, skilled cottage weavers always worked at home with their families. With the coming of computers, faxes, e-mails and the Internet more and more people are again able to work from home with their families around them - and that's surely a good and wholesome trend. Working as a family team is a good thing, something to be encouraged and reinforced wherever possible. It seems highly probable that Joseph taught Jesus his carpentry skills in their family workshop in Nazareth.

Family Workers' Poem

Working together and playing together,
Living and loving and praying together,
Being a family through each working day,
Being a family in every way:
The more that we share, then the richer we grow:
Teaching young workers what old workers know.
Sharing our skills and experience too -
You're helping me, and then I'm helping you.
Being together at work and at prayer,
Being together to love and to care.
Being together as much as we can -
The close, loving family is part of God's plan.
So help us, Great Father, in all that we do -
And may our family's work be a tribute to You.

A Prayer for those Families who Work Together

Most loving Lord, Your work of creating and sustaining this vast universe is far beyond our human comprehension. We know that Your limitless power and perfect wisdom are always at work in everything that You have made and love. Help us, in the work that we do together, to be of some small service to You, and to be a tiny part of Your Eternal Plan. Teach us to work together in love and harmony, as a happy and united family. May the things that we make, and the services we provide, be the very best of which we are capable. May we find joy and fulfilment in the work that we do together as a family, and may it be of real benefit to our brothers and sisters, as well as providing us with our daily bread. As Paul worked at his tents, and as the fishermen-disciples worked with boats and nets, so may we work in ways that are acceptable to You. We ask it in the Name of Him Who worked as a carpenter in Nazareth, Jesus Christ our Lord.

Amen.

Playing Together

It's an old and essential truth that if we pray together it can help us to stay together. It's also true that the family who make time for having fun and playing together increase their chances of staying together. Human beings are like coins: we all have two distinct sides to our personalities. We work and we play. We can be solemn and serious and we can also enjoy sheer, harmless, honest-to-goodness fun. We cannot be solely one thing or the other. We cannot be the true and complete selves God meant us to be if we are either permanently frivolous or unrelievedly grave and serious. We need to *balance* and harmonise these two discrete sides of our nature.

We can have fun with chess or draughts, with cards, with computer games, with table-tennis, cricket, rugby and soccer - or with an improvised walking-stick bat-and a discarded tennis ball the family mongrel retrieved on the beach.

Family games are for pleasure - not for prizes. Winning is unimportant. It is the joy of playing and the loving companionship that matters. Family games may well involve movable goal-posts and rules more flexible than wet spaghetti -- but they enable the young and the old, the whole and the handicapped to relax, to enjoy themselves and to laugh together.

Playing Together

I've forgotten what the score is.
I suspect that no-one cares.
The charade team's in the kitchen.
Rover's barking on the stairs.
Uncle Jack is trying to show us
How Dad's conjuring tricks are done.
Little Sally's giggling loudly.
Cousin Janet shouts: "I've won!"
Mum and Granddad in the kitchen,
Washing up and making tea.
Grandma handing home-made cakes round -
Which are eaten eagerly.
This is family fun and chaos:
This is happiness untold.
God's great gift of fun together
Is worth more than finest gold.

Prayer for Family Games

Great Lord of love and laughter, giver of every good and perfect gift, we thank and praise You now for this special gift of family fun, for the pleasure and privilege of being together and playing together. Help us to understand that relaxation and leisure, enjoyable hobbies, games and pastimes are just as important as our work. Help us to understand one another better through the games we play, the songs we sing and the jokes we share. It was Your great love for us, O Lord, which gave us the ability to relax and enjoy our leisure together as a family. Help us to make the most of it, and always to remember that You are the source of all true joy. We ask it in the Name of Christ our Lord.

Amen

Helping and Being Helped

Many years ago I worked in a big open plan office with two great pals called Ron Granger and Colin Wakefield. They were two of the best work colleagues a man could ever wish for: they always helped me whenever I needed it, and I tried to do the same for them. Sadly, Colin was struck down by multiple sclerosis which confined him to a wheel chair for many years, but his courage never deserted him, and his keen mind was as sharp as a razor right to the end. In the days when CB radios were popular he gave himself the code name Action Man, and enjoyed helping kids with their maths home-work over the air waves. He did what he could. He was always willing to help. The loving teenage niece or nephew who can't quite see the answer to an awkward quadratic equation can run an errand or two for the mathematical uncle in the wheelchair. The loving but immobile uncle can bounce Euclid off the wall and chop up differential calculus as easily as salad. God made each one of us unique. I cannot play your part and you cannot play mine. It is only when we care and share and help one another in the family - and beyond the family - that God's perfect will for the whole of His human family can be accomplished.

The Helpers' Poem

Open my eyes and mind that I may see
Those in my family in need of me.
Open my hands and heart that I may give
The help they need as long as I may live.
Teach me, O Lord, when I'm the one in need,
How to be grateful for a loving deed.
Help me appreciate each kindness shown:
All goodness flows from You, and You alone.
The kindest and most loving of our race
Is but a channel of Eternal Grace.
Flow through us Lord, unworthy though we be,
Help me help those I love, as they help me.

The Helpers' Prayer

Lord Jesus, in your parable about the Good Samaritan, You taught us that it is practical help that makes us into good neighbours. Teach us to be practical, as the Samaritan was, and to do good things to help others -- especially those in our own families who are close to us and who need our special help and love. Give us the strength to heal, nurse and care for all sick and injured family members. Grant us the patience and love to tolerate and sympathise with those whom we find wearing and difficult, remembering always that we ourselves may be difficult and wearing to others. Help us to accept help gratefully, as well as to offer it cheerfully and willingly. We ask it in the Name of Him Who helped us to the uttermost, Jesus Christ our Lord.
Amen.

Understanding One Another

After trying to understand myself for over sixty years, I still know almost nothing about the subject. If I can't even begin to understand my own personality, how can I hope to understand someone else's? Patricia and I have been married for over forty years and we knew each other long before we were married - yet we still surprise each other sometimes . . .

"I never knew you liked geraniums!"

"You never told me that joke before!"

Yet difficult as it is, true understanding is at the centre of every good, loving and enduring family relationship. There's a wise old Amerindian proverb which runs: "You should never judge a man until you have walked for a full day in his moccasins." We would all do well to take that to heart. Even if anything approaching full understanding is God's privilege alone, we have to *try* to understand. One useful tip is never to *assume*. Very few of us are telepathic. If you don't know how a family member feels about something: *ask*. It's also vitally important to express our own thoughts and feelings. Bottling and suppressing grievances - real or imagined - is usually counter-productive. Always speak lovingly and sympathetically, but speak frankly and honestly too.

Understanding One Another

"If I *were* you . . . "
"You're not! So let me be."
"But if you do as I suggest . . . "
"I'd not be my true self."
"You know I'm right."
"I don't - and even if you were,
I'd still prefer to live my life my way!"
"You're being most unreasonable."
"I know. That's how I'm made."
"Thank God for that. We're right to be ourselves,
Those precious, individual selves God gave . . .
He is a generous God."
"We must remember that next time we disagree."
"We must indeed. I love you as you are, so please don't change."

A Prayer for Understanding

Most loving and understanding Lord Jesus, You know us so well because you created us in the beginning and You sustain us now and always. Grant us a share of Your deep and loving understanding, so that we may begin to try to love and understand one another as You love and understand us. Help us to see that every man, woman and child is a unique and special personality. Help us to accept one another's differences and to realise that we are different because You planned it so.

We ask it in and through Your precious Name.

Amen.

At Home Together

One old song reminds us that there's no place like home. Another blesses every aspect of a house, and draws spiritual analogies from homely things like walls and windows. There are many nuggets of truth still waiting to be dug from those old musical mines. Jesus used familiar, homely things in His timeless parables. He visited people in their homes: Zacchaeus the tax collector, Mary and Martha at Bethany. Jesus also went to Peter's home where He healed the disciple's wife's mother of her fever. Home life is a vital part of family life. Being at home together is one of the greatest joys a human family can share. Each one of us can contribute to those deep and lasting pleasures. Each one of us can help with cleaning, decorating, tidying, enriching and beautifying the family home. We can show our appreciation of what the other members of the family are doing for the home we share, we can encourage them, assist them and praise their work. We can show them that what matters to them, a cherished pet, a souvenir teapot, picture or ornament, matters just as much to us because we love them, and so the things that are precious to them are precious to us as well because of our love. A home which is filled with family love is the ideal place to relax and unwind. We can sit there peacefully beside the people we love and quietly thank God for them.

Poem for the Family at Home Together

Brother, sister, father, mother:
Thank You, Lord, we've got each other,
Home together, loving, caring,
Listening, talking, giving, sharing.
Three course meal, or glass of water,
Brought by loving son or daughter.
Cottage, palace, house or flat,
Mobile home with welcome mat
Spread across a patch of heather:
Home is home when we're together.
Home is for my family:
I love them and they love me.

Prayer for the Family at Home Together

Lord Jesus, Your first home was a stable at Bethlehem because the inn was full. You are the unseen guest in every home from the most ornate and luxurious palace to the simplest cottage or favela. Lord of love, teach us that it is love which makes a home, and help us to follow your example of perfect love as closely as we can. Grant us the opportunity to be together at home with the family we love as often as possible. Help us to savour these precious moments of joy in this our earthly home, moments which are only foretastes of the eternal, heavenly home where we shall know perfect fellowship forever with You and with all whom we love on earth.

Amen.

On Holiday Together

There are as many different types of holiday as there are different types of people. Some of us want sun and sand. Others need action and adventure. Some of us want to relax and read, listen to the radio or watch TV. Others need to swim, work out in the gym, or swing tennis rackets and golf clubs from dawn till dusk. Some of us like to return regularly to tried and tested places. Others seek something new and exciting to explore. Some enjoy a pilgrimage to the Holy Land. Others prefer Blackpool, Yarmouth, or Southend. Patricia and I are fortunate: we both enjoy our work, and we choose working holidays together researching unexplained mysteries like the Oak Island Money Pit in Nova Scotia, or the ancient labyrinth at Knossos. Often, different family members enjoy different things, but they also want to enjoy the company of the family they love. So how is that problem solved? One answer is to pick a location which offers a wide variety of facilities close together: a well equipped gymnasium, a large swimming pool, quiet shady places to relax and read, ancient ruins to explore, theatres, cinemas and restaurants. By doing different things and then getting together again later to share the accounts of our various adventures, we can follow our own individual interests and still keep the family united.

The Family Holiday Poem

There are mountains to climb.
There are deserts to cross.
There are bustling resorts and green dales.
There are pictures to paint.
There are poems to write.
There are books full of wonderful tales.
There's so *much* we can do
But I have to have you
Close beside me or else nothing's worth.
When our family's together
Whatever the weather
We'll have the best time on God's earth!

The Family Holiday Prayer

Thank You, Holy Father, for providing us with such a wonderful world to explore and enjoy. Help us to find all the limitless holiday happiness that You intend us to have together. Guide us to places where we can all enjoy ourselves as a family, and where we can have fun, excitement and relaxation together. Help each one of us to do the individual things which he or she likes most, and then to tell the others what we have done, and listen to the accounts of what they have done with loving, caring interest. May this happy holiday time which we enjoy together give us the opportunity to grow closer in our love for one another and closer to You, the real Head of every loving family.

Amen.

Family Reunions

It needs the importance of Christmas, birthdays, anniversaries, weddings, baptisms - or the sadness of funerals -- to bring about a full scale family reunion. Giles, the brilliant cartoonist, was a keen observer of family life. He used to draw a little group of ladies in one corner and label them "Christmas Aunts " and those Giles ladies, God bless them, only managed to see one another at Christmas. It really is worth making the effort to get together more often. *Today* is an important day. Let's use it well. Let's use it for the family. Let's see whether we can arrange to get together with someone we love whom we haven't seen in a while . . . since the last wedding, the most recent baptism, perhaps since last Christmas. Family reunions are rather like recharging the batteries regularly. Love is a very powerful force, but even love needs recharging sometimes. It is only God's love which is truly inexhaustible - ours needs to be reinforced, strengthened and renewed from time to time: and family reunions are effective renewal agents. One lovely old Christian whom we knew many years ago, would sometimes look in genuine wonder at a vast crowd emerging from a busy station at rush hour, or from a football stadium after a cup match, and say: "My word, we'll be so busy in Heaven catching up with all our friends and family!"

Family Reunion Poem

We'd not seen dear old Uncle George since 1982.
The world gets busier all the time: there's such a lot to do.
George had many things to tell us, family news we hadn't heard.
We sat and listened, quite entranced, to every single word.
His daughter was a doctor, and his son a Parish Priest,
Cousin Frank a Missionary serving somewhere in the East.
Auntie Maude was busy helping in a shop for the Red Cross.
Cousin Pete had been promoted by his very grateful boss.
Every face came up in memory as we heard what they had done,
As we listened, and remembered, and thanked God for every one.
We resolved to meet more often, and to try the best we could
To hold family reunions, for we knew they'd do us good.
All of us are much too busy, working morning, noon and night:
Making time to be together is a very worthwhile fight.
Clocks and calendars -- relentlessly they wear our lives away -
With God's help we'll get together and hold Father Time at bay.

Family Reunion Prayer

Almighty Father of every family, You love each one of us, and Your will is that we should always be happily united in loving family fellowship. Help us to find the time and opportunity to be together as often as we can. Teach us to be good listeners and good communicators, sharing all our family news with love. May every man and woman, and every boy and girl in this family meet together often - and always with mutual love and respect. May we be proud of one another, and glad that we belong together; and may we always love, help and serve one another with true Christian gladness, through Jesus Christ our Lord.
Amen.

Happy Occasions

With all our sin and selfishness, and despite all our human frailty, we genuinely enjoy giving happiness to the people we love. God's love for us exceeds the noblest love we feel for one another by a factor of infinity. If the best human beings enjoy seeing the people they love happy, how much more so does God delight in our happiness? God is love, and the purest expression of love is the creation of joy for those whom we love. The innermost core, the quintessential nucleus, of all true Christianity is the realisation that Jesus came to Earth to bring us eternal and abundant life: not mere existence, nor subsistence, nothing fading, fleeting, ephemeral nor transient *but life eternal and abundant*. That is the priceless, breathtaking gift of our all-loving and all-powerful God. He never makes promises He cannot keep. His will for all His people is eternal joy beyond anything our finite, earthly minds can imagine. When we truly love another person, we want him or her with us forever. Because God loves us with a love beyond our wildest imaginings, He wants us with Him forever: and God's infinite power can never be defeated. His omnipotence equals His love. When we praise Him as our *Almighty* God, it means just that. There is no finer form of worship, no deeper kind of prayer than being happy together in the Name of the Lord.

Poem for Happy Occasions

Eternal and abundant life! Great Lord,
Bind us together with Your golden cord.
Teach us Your way of perfect joy and love,
First here on Earth, and then in Heaven above.
Happy together, seeking to give joy
To those we love, and never to annoy,
Nor thwart, deny, nor hinder happiness:
Whenever in our power, to answer "Yes."
To give our loving family all we can:
Our thoughts, our care, our time -- and always plan
To bring them some fresh joy, or some new pleasure,
A loving gift which loving hearts will treasure.
God loves us all, and He would have us be
Radiant with joy for all eternity.

Prayer for Happy Occasions

Lord of eternal and abundant life, giver of every good and perfect gift, help us to rejoice with You on every happy family occasion. Help us to rejoice in one another's presence at Christmas, on birthdays and anniversaries, at times of success and achievement. Remind us, O Lord, that all these good and happy things come from You, and make us properly grateful for them. Help us to derive our greatest and most lasting happiness from the happiness of those we love, and help us to live so that we may always contribute to it. We ask it in the Name of Christ our Lord, who came to our world that we might enjoy eternal and abundant life with Him.

Amen.

Exciting Occasions

There is nothing we enjoy more than roaring down the M4 astride our big, black Harley Davidson Electra Glide. It's like sailing, flying and surfing all rolled into one exciting experience. A Harley Davidson is not only the best motor-bike on Earth -- it's a legend on wheels. Other members of our much loved family find their excitement in different ways. They tell us about what thrills them, and we tell them about biking. That way we can share one another's excitement vicariously. It's exciting when a member of the family achieves something, passes an important examination, gets promoted, engaged, married, becomes a parent, or a grandparent, gets his or her own radio or TV show, or lands an important rôle in a new West End play. Because that family member is loved by all the others, that excitement is shared. C.S.Lewis once said that true humility is having the ability to design and build the finest cathedral in the world, to know it's the best, and then to be no more nor less pleased than if one of your family or friends had done it. True excitement is that same kind of loving, shared excitement that Lewis was talking about when he wrote of true humility. If the rest of the family can live through the excitement and enjoy it with us, that doubles it.

Poem for Exciting Occasions

There's excitement in the air,
An excitement we can share,
As our pulses start to race
Tension shows on every face:
Full of action, full of verve,
Pounding heart and tingling nerve.
All the muscles tensed like springs:
Oh what joy excitement brings!
With the family beside us
To encourage, help and guide us,
Young and old, both large and small:
Shared excitement fills us all.
Tension mounts, and eyes are lighting:
Thank You, Lord, Your world's exciting.
Thank you, Lord, that we are in it.
Thanks for each exciting minute.

Prayer for Exciting Occasions

Most loving and understanding Lord, You know our every need and every mood. We thank and praise You for tranquillity when we need peace and rest, and we thank You for all that is thrilling and exhilarating when we need excitement. Help us to enjoy every kind of good adventure together, and to share all kinds of happy and wholesome excitement with the families we love. Remind us, Lord, that even the bravest, the most confident and the most daring adventurers need the help and support of the families who love them, and most of all they need You. We ask it in the Name of Christ our Lord.
Amen.

Sad Occasions

Seasons roll on. Dark winter days follow the bright gladness of summer. Night follows day. Rain falls, and so do tears. The price of daring to love someone more than we love ourselves is the constant fear that those we love so much may be injured, or taken seriously ill, or that death will separate us from them. Families whose members love one another have to face sad occasions as well as joyful and exciting ones. It is at such times that we need one another most. There is no comfort as great as the understanding, sympathetic presence of a loving family when things have gone terribly wrong. Bereavement, serious illness, disability, failure and disappointment are all made a little less terrible when our loved ones are there with us to help us through them. God in His loving wisdom gave us our families to see us through sad, dark times, as well as to rejoice with us when all goes well. Our Lord's mother, Mary, rejoiced when Gabriel brought her the great news: standing silently at the foot of the cross she gave Jesus the loving sympathy and support of her courageous presence. Bethlehem and Calvary - infinite joy and ultimate sadness - - were both family moments. As Mary stayed with Jesus, so we must stay loyally with those we love during their darkest and saddest times.

Poem for Sad Occasions

Thank God at times like these
That he provides
The strongest families and the truest friends.
Thank God for every loving word they speak
And for the silence of companionship
That speaks by simply being there:
A gentle hand to hold,
And a strong shoulder upon which to lean.
Thank God that when the night
Is darker than the weeping soul can bear
The family's there
To comfort, love and care,
And so is He.

Prayer for Sad Occasions

Lord of Gethsemane and Calvary, be with us in this sad, dark hour. You know the fullest meaning of suffering and sadness, of pain and of death. Help and comfort us. Teach us never to give up, but to fight, to survive and to go on. Teach us to support and help one another now, when we need one another most. Grant us a portion of that strength which was in Christ during His darkest and saddest time. Teach us that this night will end in morning, that winter will turn to spring, and that the darkest storm clouds will part to reveal the glory of the sunlight once more. We ask it in the Name of Christ our Lord.

Amen.

Family Prayers and Bible Study

The Bible is a uniquely wonderful and powerful book. It has so much to teach us about God's love, about the risen and ascended Christ's glorious triumph over sin and death for our sakes, and about the way in which God wants us to treat one another as members of our own Christian families, as well as members of His one vast human family. Reading and studying the Bible prayerfully and carefully together is a vitally important Christian family activity. Family prayer is equally important. Loving our families as we do, we want to share life's greatest treasures together. Family Bible study and prayer are two of life's most precious and sublime treasures, enjoying them together can be one of our most rewarding and enriching experiences. Praying together as a family reminds us that God Himself is the true Head of our family, and of every family. Prayers and Bible study unite us with God as well as with one another. Prayers and Bible study are the deep, spiritual refreshment which our hearts, minds and spirits need as much as our physical bodies need food and drink, regular exercise and peaceful sleep. By praying and studying the Bible together as a family we are keeping our spiritual lines of communication open: we are listening to God, and speaking to Him in prayer.

Prayer and Bible Study Poem

As we turn its sacred pages,
We are carried down the ages
To the distant times of Patriarchs and Kings,
To the Prophet souls of yore -
Those who kept God's Holy Law --
As their prayers flew up to Him on silent wings.
That same Bible speaks today,
As we read it when we pray
With our loving families round us as we do.
In our world with Internet
And the supersonic jet
God's great love for us is timeless, strong and true.

The Family Bible Study Prayer

Teach us and guide us, great Lord of Eternal Truth and Wisdom. Lead us through these sacred pages and show us how to understand them. Help us to learn from what is recorded here of the history of Patriarchs and Kings, Prophets and Priests, as well as from the lives of ordinary people like ourselves. May we aim to be as fearless as David, as loyal and loving as Ruth, as enthusiastic as Peter and as calm and wise as John. Teach us to pray, as Jesus Himself taught the first Disciples to pray. We ask it in His Name.

Amen.

Worshipping Together

Just as there is a proper and essential place for family prayers and Bible study at home, so there is a proper and essential place for worshipping together as a Christian community. Our lives as members of loving Christian families teach us our need of one another in the family circle. Our lives in the wider world outside - at school, at the factory bench, in the shop, warehouse, office desk or driver's cab - teach us our need of Christian companions who can support and reinforce one another at a place of worship. It may be a small village chapel on a rugged Welsh hillside. It may be a house church, which moves from one member's home to another. It may be a vast and beautiful cathedral filled with stained glass, sacred pictures and statues. Just as every Christian man or woman is a unique individual with different personal needs, so there are different meeting places where equally sincere and acceptable worship is offered in different ways. What is ideal for one worshipper is not necessarily right for another. Our task as loving family members is to support and respect one another's ideas of worship, and to get together for combined ecumenical services as often as we can. Lionel serves as a part-time, non-stipendiary Anglican Priest: our daughters and their families are Methodists and Baptists - but we all love one another dearly.

Poem for Worshipping Together

There are those who love the incense, and the music and the bells.
Some prefer deep Quaker silence where the Holy Spirit dwells.
Some are happy in small chapels with Welsh mountains at their backs.
Some seek ancient holy places reached by steep and winding tracks.
Some like singing on street corners, praising God in open air.
Others gather in their houses, meeting fellow Christians there.
Let your church be where your heart is. What God leads you to is right.
We can praise Him in the morning. We can worship Him by night.
We can serve Him in deep silence, or when music thrills the ear.
All He asks of those who gather is that they should be sincere.

Prayer for Worshipping Together

Lord of all peoples, of every race and clime, of every man, woman and child, help us to worship and praise You together to the best of our ability. Inspire our sacred silences, our Christian music and our preaching. Help us to pray together from our hearts, and to rejoice in the loving fellowship and communion of those who share our churches, chapels, cathedrals and home-worship. Teach us to concentrate on what unites us and to be tolerant of what we find different in the worship of others. We ask it in the Name of Him Who taught us to worship You in spirit and in truth, Jesus Christ our Lord.
Amen.

Studying and Learning Together

Learning is a life-long process, and life itself is the best teaching institution. Paper qualifications are becoming increasingly fashionable as the years go by, and in contemporary society they are undeniably useful rungs on the ladder of success. Before school attendance became compulsory towards the end of Victoria's reign, almost everyone was educated at home. Only the rich could afford private schools, tutors or governesses: families did the rest -- and for thousands of years society survived perfectly well without any form of compulsory education at all -- something which today's enthusiasts for formal schooling tend to forget. It's possible to learn all you need to know outside the official educational system. Inside or outside that official system, however, studying and learning with the family is a tremendous asset for students of any age. When the people you love are studying and revising hard, at school, at college, at university or for some professional qualifications, the rest of the family does everything it can to help. You provide a quiet place for them to work. You pop out to the library or bookshop to get something they need. You keep them going with cups of tea and sandwiches, and you do their share of the housework until the vital examination is safely over. It's just another way of showing Christian family love.

Poem for Studying and Learning Together

I couldn't tackle this alone. Revision is so boring.
Though will-power tries to get me through: my body's gently snoring.
Mum's brought more tea, and Dad's has gamely volunteered to read
Because my eyes are telling me a break is what they need.
I've bitten this old ball point pen until the plastic's dented.
I wish thermo-dynamic laws had never been invented.
I know the Tudor Vagrants' Acts caused much distress and trouble,
But can't recall a single fact about the South Sea Bubble.
French, German and Geography have left my brain so weary
The continents are all confused in my tectonic theory.
But Mum and Dad and all my team are doing what they do:
My family are with me and they're going to pull me through.
As well as helping all they can, I know they often pray:
"God bless each candidate who sits for an exam today."

54

Prayer for Studying and Learning Together

Wisest Lord, You are the Designer, Maker and Sustainer of this infinite universe. All its vast distances, immense powers, complicated systems and abstract principles are very simple and basic to You. Help us to study it together as a Christian family and to learn a little more about it every day, so that as we understand more and more of the wonders of the cosmos, we may come to realise afresh Your infinite power and wisdom as its Creator and Sustainer. We ask it in the Name of Him Who was there with You in the beginning, and Who shared in Your great work of creation, Jesus Christ our Lord.
Amen.

Sharing Hobbies and Interests

Our hobbies and leisure interests help us to establish our individuality. Some of us collect stamps, coins and medals. Others appreciate Staffordshire pottery. Aunt Joan is always busy in the garden. Grandfather is a keen fisherman. Uncle Walter draws and paints. Sister Anthea is a wood carver and turner. Brother Dennis likes cooking Chinese meals. We are attracted to making things, collecting things, and doing things. When members of the family enjoy different hobbies, they can explain their special interests to the others and so share their pleasures. As loving members of Christian families, we owe it to one another to explain our own special hobbies to the others, and then to listen with genuine interest and attention while they tell us about theirs. Our favourite hobbies and leisure interests can take us out of ourselves. When our thoughts are in danger of turning inwards, when we are feeling sorry for ourselves, becoming depressed, or grumbling about trivia, our hobbies and pastimes can be very helpful - and those that we can do together are the most beneficial. The finest leisure interests of all are the ones that help others: things like voluntary work in a charity shop, or learning first aid and being available when those special life-saving skills are needed.

Hobbies and Interests Poem

Let's walk together over open dales,
The Scottish islands or the hills of Wales.
Show me those stamps with their Victoria heads.
Teach me the watermarks of Penny Reds.
How was this medal won in the Crimea?
Such fascinating porcelain! What's its year?
Explain the way that crossword clue was solved.
To learn your skill at chess I'm now resolved.
What's this red flower called? And that tall tree?
Please share your knowledge of these things with me.
Good hobbies always make a joy of leisure,
But doing them together's what we treasure.
We multiply their pleasure and their zest
By making each a family interest.

Prayer for Sharing Hobbies and Interests

Lord, You are the Creator of all true and loving companionship, help us to use our hobbies and interests to unite this loving family and bring us ever closer together. Give us the grace to take a deep and genuine interest in all the things that those we love enjoy doing. Help us to listen carefully to what they tell us, and assist us to appreciate the things they show us. Preserve us from being boring when we tell them about our own special interests in return. Teach us to find things that we can all enjoy doing together and to concentrate on those special interests in which *every* member of the family can be included. We ask it in the Name of Jesus our Lord.
Amen.

Listening, Talking and Communicating

Sometimes when we speak, no-one seems to take any notice. We listen and ignore what we're hearing because the speaker isn't saying what we hoped to hear. Communication occurs when people speak the simple truth in love, and their listeners think carefully about what is being said - even if they don't agree with it. Voltaire didn't quite say what he's usually credited with saying, but the gist of his words was that although he might disagree vehemently with a speaker he would staunchly defend that person's right to speak. One of the worst and most destructive family errors is to try to plan another member's life. Avoid it like the smoking crater of an active volcano. It is arrogant and presumptuous to think that we know better than someone else. Only in the most exceptional circumstances should we dare to offer advice before the person we love requests it. The deepest and most loving communication need not be verbal. A broad smile, a comforting arm around the shoulder, or taking a loved one's hand, can sometimes say more than the most carefully selected words. Families are the ideal settings in which to communicate -- tragically, we don't always do it effectively. Clear communication is a vital part of loving Christian family fellowship: we have to get it right.

Poem for Communicators

My heart is filled with love for you,
My family and my friends.
But how can we communicate
This love that never ends?
A word may help, a gentle touch,
A gift, a smile, a tear.
What can we think, or say, or do
For those we hold so dear?
If thoughts could leap from mind to mind,
And love from heart to heart,
Then we could still express our love
Although we were apart.
The joys of Heaven lie ahead
Where round God's glorious throne
We shall communicate our love
And know as we are known.

The Communicators' Prayer

Most wise and loving God, Your communication alone is perfect, whereas ours so often fails. We can rarely find the best words or actions with which to express our love for the family members whom we care for so much. Grant us the wisdom to communicate with our families effectively. Help us to watch, to listen and to understand the needs, the hopes, and the fears of others. Inspire us to do and say exactly what's needed at the most appropriate time. Teach us to look beneath the surface things, and to find the deepest needs of those we love, so that we can help them to achieve what they really want. We ask it in the Name of Christ our Lord Who communicated His eternal truth perfectly by His Cross and Resurrection.
Amen.

Agreeing to Disagree

This is one of the great central pillars upon which family life rests. We not only need to love one another in the family situation - we need to respect one another as well. We have to accept that the wisest and most experienced family member does not have a permanent monopoly on truth, or on good new ideas. We have to disagree sometimes, but disagreeing is not the same as quarrelling nor arguing. Disagreeing is having the strength of mind and character to say: "I love and respect you with all my heart, but what may be right for you on this occasion, just isn't right for me." Lord Soper used to speak for Christ in the open air on Tower Hill and at the Hyde Park Speakers' Corner. A regular heckler on these occasions was a diminutive cockney atheist, with a great line in repartee. It was a real education to hear the two of them going at it as hard as they could. But at the end of the argument, the little cockney would produce a tin of throat lozenges and offer them to Soper, who always accepted one gracefully. He referred to their sparkling verbal duels as the *fellowship of controversy* - and he was absolutely right. Those two highly intelligent and strong-minded men could always agree to disagree, and each of them greatly liked and admired the other.

Poem for Those who can Agree to Disagree

I cannot in a million years accept your point of view,
But you're my brother and my friend - and I can accept you.
There is no ground that I can give, and you will not retreat.
There is no honest compromise, nor bridge where we can meet.
Our ideas clash like sword on shield, and so it seems to me,
The only common ground we've got: "Agree to disagree!"
You're more to me, my kinsman, than as yet you've ever known.
Ideas are insubstantial things - but we are flesh and bone.
The Christian family must hold fast, and in God's name unite.
There's evil out there in the world: that's what we've got to
fight.
We disagree on several things - perhaps we always will -
But in God's eyes and in our own we can be brothers still.

Prayer for Those who Agree to Disagree

Lord of harmony and love, help us never to insert an argument or a point of view as a dangerous barrier between ourselves and other members of our greatly loved Christian families. We need never compromise important principles, because perfect love and unselfish fellowship are the highest Christian principles of all. Give us tolerance, O Lord, and the humility to accept that there are times when we could be wrong. Help us to love those family members who disagree with us, and help them to love us in turn when we disagree with them. We ask it in and through the precious Name of Jesus Christ our Lord. Amen.

Family Priorities

On this last page of our book, we'd like to try to summarise our central theme of Christian love manifested in the Christian family, because it's been our own personal experience since 1957 that the strength, warmth and security of a loving Christian family is the greatest gift God gives us this side of Heaven. Our first priority is to praise and thank God for the institution of the Christian family and for our own joyful experience of it.

Our second priority is to resolve to think positively about every much-loved member of the family, to see how we can best be of use to them and bring them all the happiness we can. Our third priority is our duty to the wider community of which our family is a part: we need to be an outgoing, socially responsible family, playing our part in that wider community, and doing our very best to help those in need. Our fourth priority is to ourselves. We have the same rights and privileges as the brothers, sisters and family members whom it is our loving duty to serve. By putting God first and them second, we, ourselves, do not merely vanish away like mist in wind and sun. As the brilliant C.S.Lewis once wrote: "When we have learned to love our neighbours as ourselves, we may then begin to love ourselves as much as we love our neighbours."